I Was Wondering

Where Do the Leaves Go?

It was a beautiful, crisp fall day. The Cahans were out hiking in the woods. Aaron was enjoying the swishing noise his feet made as he dragged them through the thick layer of leaves that had fallen to the ground.

"I'm sure glad we don't have to rake all *these* leaves," he said to his sisters. "Where do you suppose they go when no one rakes them up?"

Have you ever wondered what happens to the millions of leaves that fall from the trees each autumn? Aaron's sisters, Ellen and Claire, are real nature lovers. They told him all about what happens to leaves when they fall.

At this time of year water can no longer
flow to the leaves. A connection point
between tubes that carry water to the
leaves, and the leaves themselves, seals up.
Without water, the leaves die and fall. If
these leaves kept piling up year after year,
we'd have a huge heap of leaves. The small
plants, animals, and insects that live near
the ground would be smothered. But, as you
may have guessed, the leaves don't lie on
the ground forever. They become food for
insects, other plants, and eventually for the
very tree from which they fell.

Leaves contain many nutritious
minerals—calcium, iron, phosphorus, and
potassium, for example. As the leaves lie on
the ground and become wet with rain, the
bacteria in the soil use them for food. This is

water
tubes

called decay. Some small insects eat the soft parts of dead leaves. All this chomping and chewing and decaying breaks the leaves down, leaving the important minerals to seep slowly into the soil. When the spring rains come, this precious food is carried to the roots of nearby plants, which are now hungry after their long winter's rest.

"See . . . ," Ellie told Aaron, "although the leaves 'leave' their tree, they give back something very important—food."

"Why do we have to rake the leaves, then?" Aaron asked. "Why can't we just leave them to feed the grass?"

"We could," Claire answered. "But they'd look too messy."

"Or we could make a compost pile," suggested Ellie. "You make a flat pile of leaves, grass, and other natural things and leave it. This stuff will decay and turn it into a kind of fertilizer. You can put it on the lawn or in the garden to help the grass and plants grow better."

"A great idea!" Aaron declared. "I think you two should be in charge of lawn cleanup."

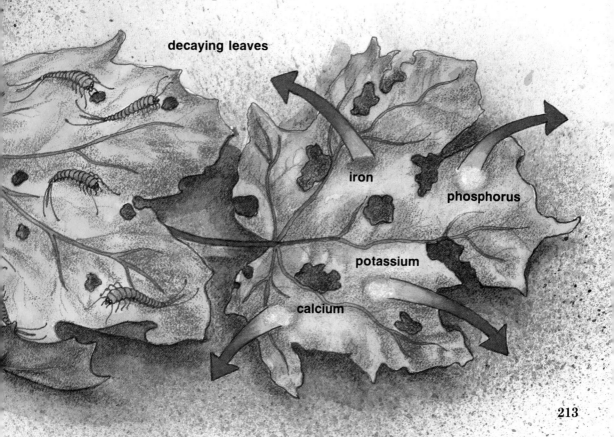

decaying leaves

iron

phosphorus

potassium

calcium

How does composting work?

1. Have Mom or Dad help you pick an out-of-the-way corner in your backyard, or somewhere else, about 3 square feet (.8 square meter).

Things you need:
backyard corner
garden shovel
water
grass clippings
leaves
dead plants
vegetable or fruit peels

2. Collect a pile of "nature's leftovers": grass clippings, twigs, fallen leaves, dead plants, and other things like these. Put them in the compost patch.

3. Mix the fruit and vegetable peels in the pile. Sprinkle water over the mixture.

4. Turn up the mixture each month with the shovel. The compost pile will need a few months, and it will break down into smaller bits of natural material called compost.

5. You can mix the compost into garden soil. It will help return minerals to the soil and keep new plants healthy.

*Get permission first.

Why Don't Trees Die in Winter?

"It's cold!" Lee announced, shivering at the bus stop. "I'm glad I don't have to stand out here all winter like this poor maple tree."

"How do you suppose they do it?" Zach asked. "Winter is really cold, but every spring they always come back—the trees and bushes always get leaves, the flowers always sprout, and Mrs. Polchek's roses always bloom. Why don't they die during the winter? I know I would."

Lee and Zach did some detective work in the school library. They learned some interesting things about plants.

The aboveground parts of many small plants actually do die, but the parts

underground stay alive. These parts store food that the plant made during the summer growing season. They go into a resting state like many animals do during the winter. When spring comes, the stored-up food is used to feed the new stems and leaves that sprout.

Other plants die completely—both above and below the ground. But they leave their seeds behind, which also rest in the frozen ground. Most of these seeds have a hard covering, so they are not damaged by the harsh weather. They start new plants when the ground warms up in the spring.

Large woody plants like trees stay alive above as well as below the ground, but they

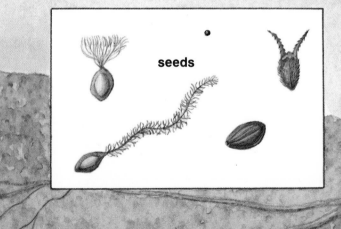

roots

seeds

buds

also go into a resting state. Their cells
change so that water will not freeze inside
the tree and damage it. Cells are the tiny
parts that make up a tree, or any living
thing. The trees have stored food in their
roots, trunks, and branches. They already
have buds that will be next year's leaves.
The buds are tightly closed, however, and
are covered by scales that keep them moist
and protected.

"I have a sure-fire idea for a winning
science project," Zach told Lee. "Let's wrap
you tightly in scales and see who survives
the winter better—you or the maple tree."

"Very funny, wise guy," Lee replied.
"Just keep reading."

What Makes Wild Plants Wild?

Have you ever seen a dandelion rising from the tiniest crack in a sidewalk? Or Queen Anne's lace growing along a country road? Have you noticed a sprig of goldenrod poking up among the rubble in an empty lot? Or how about a tall sunflower sprouting in the alley behind your garage? How did these plants get there? Who planted them?

The truth is no person planted these green shoots. We say they grow wild. If they

Dandelion seeds float through the air like parachutes.

have flowers, if they're pretty, and if they brighten the landscape, we call them wild flowers. If they grow in Farmer Brown's cornfield, in Mrs. Adler's beautiful lawn, in Grandpa's rose garden, or anywhere we don't want them, we call them weeds. But they are a hearty group—real survivors. How do they do it without our help?

The secret is travel. Seeds are probably carried most often by the wind. Some plants like dandelions, milkweed, and cottonwood trees have feathery, umbrellalike seeds. Others have winged seeds, or fruits, like the maple tree. These can be carried off on a gusty day. If conditions are right, the seeds will sprout where they land.

Then there's water travel. Seeds or soil containing seeds can be washed downhill during a rainstorm. A stream or river might carry seeds to a new spot. Or take the coconut. When ripe coconuts fall from a coconut palm at the seashore, they may fall into the ocean. Currents might carry them many miles (kilometers) to another shore.

Animals are great seed carriers. Some seeds have spikes or hooks that catch on an animal's fur or feathers. The animal might travel a fair distance before the seed falls off. Birds and other animals eat the fruits of some plants and then drop the seeds in a distant spot. Squirrels often bury nuts or seeds and then forget about them. Some might sprout.

People, too, help seeds travel. Have you ever found your shoes coated with mud after playing outside? Do you suppose there were seeds hidden in that mud? Perhaps some of these seeds dropped off as you walked along. Wild plants will do anything for a ride to a new home. And once they get there, they will struggle hard to stay alive. With rain and sunshine, usually they'll do just fine.

Wild Strawberries

A re Wild Strawberries really wild?
  Will they scratch an adult, will they snap at a child?
Should you pet them, or let them run free where they roam?
Could they ever relax in a steam-heated home?
Can they be trained not to growl at the guests?
Will a litterbox work or would they leave a mess?
Can we make them a Cowberry, herding the cows,
Or maybe a Muleberry pulling the plows,
Or maybe a Huntberry chasing the grouse,
Or maybe a Watchberry guarding the house,
And though they may curl up at your feet oh so sweetly,
Can you ever feel that you trust them completely?
Or should we make a pet out of something less scary,
Like the Domestic Prune or the Imported Cherry,
Anyhow, you've been warned and I will not be blamed
If your Wild Strawberry cannot be tamed.

—Shel Silverstein

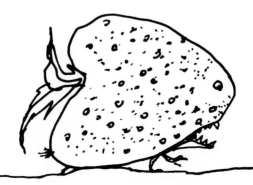

What Is Bark For?

"I sure could do without the bumpy bark on this old tree," Katie muttered to herself as she struggled to attach a big ribbon to the huge locust tree in front of the school. The ribbons were a reminder of school elections.

"Yes, but I can't," a deep voice answered. The voice seemed to come from the tree, but Katie knew better than to believe in talking trees. "I need my tough outer bark," the tree continued. "It's hard and waterproof and protects my soft inner wood from bugs,

I need my bark.

animals, heat, cold, and disease. A very thick outer bark can even protect us trees from forest fire."

Katie just stared and listened. So the tree went on. "If too much bark gets stripped off or eaten away by hungry animals in winter,

the food tubes just beneath the bark will be broken and I might die. As I grow, my outer bark cracks and splits or peels off. But I'm always growing new bark. It's a great bodyguard. I don't go anywhere without it."

Suddenly, a head poked out from behind the huge tree and winked.

"I knew it was you, Mr. Duncan," Katie sighed with relief. "All I did was tie a ribbon on this tree and I got a whole science lesson. That'll teach me to 'bark' up the wrong tree!"

I Wonder What This Is.

Clue: I may seem to be just standing there all day, but I'm really working hard.
Find the answer on page 245.

Why Do Some Flowers Smell Sweet?

Is it a beautiful day outside? Then take a deep breath of fresh air. Smell anything? Chances are, if it's spring or summer, you've had a whiff of some sweet-smelling flowers. They sure do make spring and summer a nice time to be outdoors. Is that really why flowers smell sweet, for our enjoyment? Have you ever wondered about this?

Flowers have their own reason for giving off such pleasant smells. It's really a way of attracting insects. And why would flowers want to attract pesty insects? Well, to flowers insects aren't pesty at all. Some flowers need insects for pollination (pohl ih NAY shuhn). Pollination is one way flowers make seeds. For a flower to be pollinated, it needs pollen from another flower of the same kind. And what is pollen? It's that powdery material in a flower, usually a golden-yellow. The most likely creatures to do the job of pollination are small ones such as bees, wasps, flies, butterflies, moths, and beetles.

Flowers make nectar, a sweet, sticky liquid of mostly sugar and water. This nectar is found deep in the flower. Insects, most often bees, are attracted by this sweet scent, as well as by the bright colors of many flowers. They dig deep into the flower

See the pollen sticking to the bee (above)? The bee will drop the pollen as it darts to other flowers, helping to form new seeds. Butterflies look for nectar, but they also carry pollen.

for the nectar—or sometimes it's actually the pollen they're after. The flower's loose pollen rubs off on their legs and bodies. When they travel to another flower for more nectar, some pollen will drop off and perhaps pollinate that flower.

Did you know that certain insects are only attracted to certain flowers? Take moths, for example. Flowers that are pollinated by moths give off their strongest smells in the evening. Because moths are night creatures with a strong sense of smell, they are quickly guided to their nectar treat in the dark.

Some flowers—those of many grasses and trees, for example—do not have sweet smells. They are pollinated by the wind and don't need to attract insects. Other flowers do smell—but not sweet. In fact, some have a downright rotten smell. These flowers, like the giant Rafflesia flowers that grow in tropical Asia, attract flies with their evil odor. The flies then pollinate the flowers.

What's that, you say? A bee on your nose? Maybe it smells Nippy Nectar Bubble Gum. Get your head back in . . . quick!

How does water travel up plants?

1. Fill each glass about one-fourth with water. Add 5-6 drops of red food coloring to one glass and 5-6 drops of blue coloring to the other. Mix.

Things you need:
white carnation flower
red and blue food
   coloring
cutting knife
two glasses
water
spoon

2. Have a grown-up slice the end off the carnation stem, and then carefully slice the stem up the middle to about one inch (2.5 centimeters) below the flower.

3. Put one-half of the stem in the blue water, and the other half in the red water.

4. Leave the flower overnight. What happens? Your blossom should get some blue and red streaks from the colored water. Water is soaked up through tubes in the stem similar to the way a paper towel soaks up liquid.

*Get permission first.

Mold: Plant or Animal?

Have you ever seen white-green mold
growing on a forgotten orange in the
refrigerator, or on a piece of old bread?
What is this thing called mold?

Think for a moment. Although mold may
seem to creep over the bread as it grows
larger, it doesn't really move on its own as
animals do. It can't really be an animal. Is it
a plant? It has no roots, stems, leaves, or
flowers. Most important, it has no leaves
and no way to make its own food as green
plants do.

Mold used to be called a plant, but now
scientists put it in a special group of living

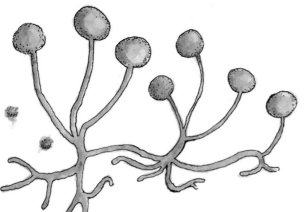

Spores, greatly enlarged here, break away from one mold and form another if conditions are right.

things called fungi (FUHN jy). Mold does not need bright sunlight. But it must take food from other living things. It does this by growing on things that can give it nourishment. Molds can grow on the foods we eat. But it can also grow on things we don't eat—like sweaty sneakers or damp laundry thrown in the closet—or on rotting leaves and logs.

Molds start from a spore. Spores act something like a seed. They will break away from one mold plant and float through the air. If a spore lands where there is just the right food and moisture, it will begin to grow. That one spore will send out threadlike runners. These runners act like roots that soak up food. They spread, making a larger mold.

So put those sneakers out to dry. Moldy sneakers are not fashionable.

How Can We Eat Fungi?

The molds you just read about are fungi. So is
mildew. But the fungi you know best are mushrooms.
They pop up like little umbrellas in the grass. Or they
cluster together at the bottom of a tree. They're even
in the grocery store—for sale, that is. Many
mushrooms are fit for eating, and they offer vitamins
and minerals. Some mushrooms are very poisonous.
So *never* taste a mushroom you find growing outside,
because you can't be sure what kind it is. But you can
be sure of one thing: These odd living things called
fungi, though they cannot produce their own food,
may come back to us as food. Sometimes nature
works that way.

Is It Alive?

adapted from Hobie Hanson, You're Weird,
by Jamie Gilson

*Eugene is absent on the last day of school, so
Hobie and Nick have to clean out his locker.
What an opportunity awaits within—
especially since their teacher, Mr. Star, has a
good sense of humor! And especially since the
class is having a birthday party for Mr. Star
anyway. Here's how Hobie tells the story.*

Eugene had locker number 37, next to
Rolf's. It was mess city. Out of the
bottom we dragged a stiff winter boot, a
strap without a backpack, a mountain of old
math sheets, lots of Band-Aid wrappers with
the little red strings hanging off, and a Hills
Brothers coffee can filled with those
markers that smell like the color they are.
Its lid was poked full of holes, like the
markers inside were hamsters and had to
breathe.

Then, on the top shelf of the locker,
under a wadded-up red Central School sweat

shirt, we found this shoebox. Eugene had written on it in grape marker, "Keep in a dark place." It was dark in the top of his locker, all right, and there was a funny smell.

We put the box on the floor and sat down and opened it.

It's a good thing we were sitting. If we hadn't been, what we found in the box would have knocked us over.

"Is it alive?" Nick asked.

"Alive and growing bigger every day," I told him. "I think it's moving."

"Will it kill you?"

"I'm not sure," I said. "Probably not unless you eat it, and I, for one, am not going to."

We both knew what it was, though. It was a birthday present for Mr. Star.

"It stinks a little," Nick said.

"It smells like what it is, that's all," I told him, holding the box out at arm's length and wishing my arm was longer.

In the box was a science experiment. A couple of months before, Mr. Star had given each of us a piece of bread. Some of us were supposed to put our bread in the refrigerator. Some of us put it in the sun.

Some of us had to rub the bread on the

floor, sprinkle it with water, and hide it in a dark place. That's the group Eugene had been in, the dirt and dark group. But he must have been absent when everybody brought their bread to class and discovered that dirt and dark made things grow on bread that sun and cold don't—spidery, gaggish threads of mold. All the D & D slices we'd looked at were disgusting after one week. Eugene's bread had been hiding out for two *months*.

We left Eugene's locker open to prove it was empty and ready for someone in next year's fourth grade. Then we carried the box back into the room.

I settled down under the back table with Eugene's purple marker and graped in the whole top of the shoebox. When I was finished, you couldn't read "Keep in a dark place" at all. Didn't look bad, and the marker smell almost killed the stink of the stuff inside. I put the box on Mr. Star's desk at the right moment and moved around to the other side of the room.

"Uh," Nick said, fairly loud, "Mr. Star, there's something on your desk." Nick didn't exactly say it was a birthday present, and

he didn't exactly say it was from him and me either.

"You *got* him something?" Molly asked, looking at the freshly markered box. "No fair."

Mr. Star smiled, all warm and kindly, as though he thought maybe this box had some homemade chocolate chip cookies, or a new tie that glowed in the dark. He looked so pleased that I began to feel sick.

"This is very thoughtful of you, class," Mr. Star said, eyeing the purple-topped box.

"It's from *all* of us," Molly said loud before Mr. Star had a chance to lift the lid. She wasn't going to let Nick and me get away with giving Mr. Star a purple present when she didn't have anything to give him.

Nick sighed, like he was mad about it but what else could he do. "Sure, OK," he said.

"The whole room," I agreed.

Everybody gathered around close to watch Mr. Star open the class gift.

Kids leaned in to look, and as he lifted off the top there was this huge group gasp. They'd expected, maybe, double-fudge-mint brownies.

"Gr-oss!" Marshall said. And I guess maybe that was the word for it. The creepy gray hairs of ancient mold had just about

239

dissolved the bread they grew on and filled up all the corners of the box. You couldn't imagine that the gooey mess at the bottom had once been something that you could spread peanut butter and jelly on.

"This is . . . astonishing," Mr. Star said. "I want you to know that in all my years of teaching. . . . " He shook his head and then, suddenly, smiled big. " . . . I've never seen a more splendid specimen of bread mold. It's outstanding. Just look at that. It's museum quality." He *liked* that box. He really *liked* it. Then grinning, he started to do a kind of silly dance. "Happy birthday to meee," he sang. Almost all the kids groaned and looked away. It's embarrassing to watch your teacher show off. "Four B is hi-is-sto-ry," he sang on.

This time everybody cheered. "Four B is you-ur sto-ry," Mr. Star sang on, even louder. "You *all* have great summers, if you don't skin your knee." At that, all the kids clapped and yelled, "All *right!*"

What other adventures did Hobie have that summer? Find out by reading Hobie Hanson, You're Weird *by Jamie Gilson.*

Answers to "I Wonder What This Is."

from page 43 Would you believe those are two hairs, very close up, on page 43 in that picture? Those rough edges you see are overlapping scales of keratin.

from page 56 Take another look. This is the Mississippi River, closer in. The photo on page 56 was taken from space with film sensitive to *infrared* rays, or heat rays. The film can record infrared rays given out by objects on the earth's surface.

from page 131   A swirl of water on a technicolor ocean?
That bright red whirl is really Planet Jupiter's famous Red
Spot, shown as the oval shape in this full view of the planet.
Most scientists believe the spot is swirling gases in Jupiter's
atmosphere.

from page 171   Those frosty crystals that look
as if they are floating in the air are really part
of a larger window frost pattern, shown above.

from page 188 That "necklace" is a spider's web laden with morning dew. Here, the spider puts finishing touches on the web as it waits for the "catch" of the day.

from page 225 Bark would have to be as rugged and tough as you see on page 255 to do its job protecting poplar trees, as shown here, or other kinds of trees.

Books to Read

Books help us satisfy our curiosity and make us more curious about ourselves and the world around us. You may find the books in this list, and others in your school or public library.

Ages 5-8

I'm Too Small, You're Too Big by Judy Barrett (Atheneum, 1981)

Friendly and funny, this book gives an important message: Although children may be too small to do some of the things that grown-ups do, grown-ups are too big to do many of the things that children do.

Learn While You Scrub: Science in the Tub by James Lewis (Simon & Schuster, 1989)

Taking a bath can be educational! All you need is a bathtub, some everyday objects that are already in your home, and . . . . Ready! Set! Into the bath you Go!

People by Peter Spier (Doubleday, 1980)

This book travels the world and tells the story of different ways people around the world do the same kinds of things.

The Seasons of Arnold's Apple Tree by Gail Gibbons (Harcourt Brace Jovanovich, 1984)

Each season brings its own wonder and pleasures. Read about and see how each new season brings a change of light, color, temperature, and activities by seeing and reading about Arnold and his apple tree. *Weather Words* is another book by Gibbons that may be of interest to you.

Snow on Bear's Nose by Jennifer Bartoli (Albert Whitman, 1976)

This book tells the story of a bear cub's first winter. Not sleepy, the cub ventures out to see and experience the winter. Just as the cub has had enough, the mother bear finds him and they go back to the den to hibernate.

What Makes It Rain? The Story of a Raindrop by Keith Brandt (Troll, 1982)

Learn how the water on earth becomes the water in rain clouds that falls back down to make puddles, ponds, and pools. This book explains the water cycle clearly, and leaves the reader amazed by the wonder of water.

Ages 9-12

A Forest Year by Carol Lerner (William Morrow and Company, 1987)

Read about how the forest animals adapt to the changes in the seasons. The illustrations show many things that we could not ordinarily see.

Gee, Wiz! by Linda Allison and David Katz (Brown Paper School Book, 1983)

Learn by doing. Seeing is believing. These common sayings are behind the fun experiments that you can find in this book.

How Did We Find Out About Sunshine? by Isaac Asimov (Walker and Company, 1987)

People did not always know what we know today. Read this book to find out what people used to think, and how we found out what we know about the sun today. Other books in this series include *How Did We Find Out About the Universe?* and *How Did We Find Out About Life in the Deep Sea?*

The Magic School Bus Lost in the Solar System by Joanna Cole (Scholastic, 1990)

Ms. Frizzle's class is supposed to go to the planetarium, but when they get there, it's closed. However, they do get to go somewhere, and the first stop is the moon! Take other field trips by reading *The Magic School Bus Inside the Human Body* and *The Magic School Bus Inside the Earth.*

Rainbows, Mirages and Sundogs: The Sky as a Source of Wonder by Roy Gallant (Macmillan, 1987)

Read more about rainbows, why the sky is blue, how to watch an eclipse safely, and other wonders.

Seasons by Melvin Berger (Doubleday, 1990)

The seasons give life on earth a natural cycle. Find out how life on earth is connected to the changing seasons. The seasons not only affect what we do, they affect what we wear and the holidays we celebrate.

Tornado by Arnold Adoff (Delacorte Press, 1977)

In a poem, Adoff tells what happened when a tornado struck an Ohio town.

Where the Waves Break: Life at the Edge of the Sea by Anita Malnig (Carolrhoda Books, 1985)

Bring underwater life to your home without getting wet. Simply find this clearly written, awesomely photographed book. After reading it, you will know what life at the edge of the sea is like.

Why Doesn't the Earth Fall Up? and Other Not So Dumb Questions About Motion by Vicki Cobb (Lodestar, 1989)

Learn about the laws of motion in this fun and informative book. It answers such questions as "Why does a rolling ball stop rolling?" and "What is a swinging object good for?"

New Words

Here are some words you have met in this book. Some of them may be new to you. Next to each word, you'll see how to say the word: **eclipse** (ih KLIHPS). The part in capital letters is said more loudly than the rest of the word. One or two sentences tell the word's meaning as it is used in this book.

atmosphere (AT muh sfihr) The atmosphere is all the air that surrounds the earth.

capillaries (KAP uh lehr eez) Capillaries are blood vessels too small to be seen. Blood vessels carry blood, and capillaries carry blood to larger vessels such as veins and arteries.

carbon dioxide (KAHR buhn dye AHX eyed) Carbon dioxide is a gas that makes up a small part of the earth's atmosphere. People and animals exhale carbon dioxide as they breathe out.

cell (sehl) A cell is the tiniest part of any living thing. The human body is made up of millions of cells.

compost (KAHM pohst) Compost is partly decayed plant material that is used as fertilizer.

condense (kuhn DEHNS) To condense is to change from a gas, such as water vapor, to a liquid, such as water, by cooling.

continental shelf (kahn tih NEHN tuhl SHEHLF) The continental shelf is the land at the edges of continents that extends down under the ocean.

core (kawr) The core of the earth is the deepest part, which is made out of very hot metals. There is an inner core and an outer core.

corona (kuh ROH nuh) The corona is the outer layer of the sun's atmosphere, which can be seen during a total eclipse.

crust (kruhst) The earth's crust is its outer rock covering, made up of the continents and the ocean floor.

earthquake (URTH kwayk) An earthquake is the shaking of the earth caused by the movement of the earth's crust.

eclipse (ih KLIHPS) An eclipse is the shadowing of one object by another in space. The moon's shadow can darken the sun. The earth's shadow can darken the moon.

erosion (ih ROH zhuhn) Erosion is the wearing away and shifting of rocks and soil on the earth's surface. Wind and water can cause erosion.

evaporate (ih VAP uh rayt) A liquid evaporates when heat changes it into a gas, such as when water dries and forms water vapor.

exhale (EHKS hayl) To exhale means to breathe out.

follicle (FAWL ih kuhl) A follicle is the opening in the skin from which hair grows.

fossil (FAHS uhl) A fossil is the print or the remains of a plant or animal that lived long ago, usually found in rock.

fungi (FUHN jy) Fungi are a group of living things that are not classified as plants. Fungi include mushrooms and molds.

galaxy (GAL uhk see) A galaxy is a group of stars, dust, and gas held together by gravity. Our galaxy, which includes our solar system, is called the Milky Way.

gills (gihlz) Gills are the breathing organs in fish and other underwater creatures. The gills work by taking oxygen from the water so that the fish can breathe.

glacier (GLAY shuhr) A glacier is a huge river of ice sliding slowly over the land.

gravity (GRAV uh tee) Gravity is the force that pulls objects toward the earth or, in outer space, toward other objects in the universe.

hibernation (hy buhr NAY shuhn) Hibernation is the long winter sleep that some animals use as a way to survive cold weather.

horizon (huh RY zuhn) The horizon is the imaginary line in the distance where the earth and sky seem to meet.

lava (LAH vuh) Lava is magma, melted rock, that bursts through the earth's surface during a volcanic eruption.

magma (MAG muh) Magma is hot, melted rock beneath the earth's crust.

mantle (MAN tuhl) The mantle is the layer of rock between the earth's crust and the outer core.

melanin (MEHL uh nihn) Melanin is the substance that produces freckles on skin.

microbe (MY krohb) A microbe is a tiny living thing, or organism, too small to be seen without a microscope. It is also called a microorganism.

microorganism (my kroh AWR ghun izm) A microorganism is a tiny living thing, too small to be seen without a microscope. It is also called a microbe.

mineral (MIHN ur uhlz) A mineral is one of thousands of nonliving materials found in rocks and soil. Gold and the graphite used to make pencils write are examples of minerals.

particles (PAHR tuh kuhlz) Particles are tiny bits of matter, such as pollen and dust.

penumbra (pih NUHM brah) The penumbra is the shadow cast during a partial eclipse.

plateau (pla TOH) A plateau is a large, raised section of land.

plates (playtz) Plates are large sections of the earth's crust that scientists believe slide over the earth's mantle.

pollination (pohl uh NAY shuhn) Pollination is the transfer of pollen from one flower to another, sometimes by insects.

rotate (ROH tayt) To rotate is to turn, as the earth rotates to change from day to night, night to day.

sediment (SEHD uh muhnt) Sediment is small bits of matter, such as rock, clay, and tiny animal bones, that build up on the earth's crust.

umbra (UHM brah) The umbra is the center of a shadow cast during a total eclipse.

volcano (vahl KAY noh) A volcano is an opening in the earth's surface, through which lava, rock, and gas burst forth. *Volcano* can also mean a mountain formed by a volcanic eruption.

Illustration Acknowledgments

The publishers of *Childcraft* gratefully acknowledge the courtesy of the following photographers, agencies, and organizations for illustrations in this volume. When all the illustrations for a sequence of pages are from a single source, the inclusive page numbers are given. Credits should be read from left to right, top to bottom, on their respective pages. All illustrations are the exclusive property of the publishers of *Childcraft* unless names are marked with an asterisk (*).

Cover: Aristocrat, Discovery, and Standard
    Bindings - Yoshi Miyake
    Heritage Binding - © Gianni Tortoli, Science Source
    from Photo Researchers*; Roberta Polfus;
    © H. Reinhard, OKAPIA from Photo Researchers*;
    Yoshi Miyake; Len Ebert; Yoshi Miyake; Roberta Polfus;
    © Barry Hennings, Photo Researchers*
  1: Joan Holub
  2-3: Yoshi Miyake
  5: Lydia Halverson
  6-7: Robert Alley
  9: Yoshi Miyake
  10-11: © Stewart Cohen, Index/Stock*
  12-15: Michele Noiset
  16-19: Dora Leder
  21: Dennis Hockerman
  22: © Nicholas DeVore III, Photographers Aspen*
  25-31: Julie Durrell
  33: © Barry Hennings, Photo Researchers*
  34-37: Julie Durrell
  38: Len Ebert
  39-40: Lydia Halverson
  41: Len Ebert
  42: Lydia Halverson
  43: CNRI/SPL from Photo Researchers*
  44: Lydia Halverson; Len Ebert
  45-49: Eileen Mueller Neill
  50-51: © Michael J. Howell, Index/Stock*
  52-55: Robert Alley
  56: NASA from Photo Researchers/Science Source*
  57: Toni Hormann
  58-59: Roberta Polfus
  60-61: © Emil Schulthess, Black Star*
  62-66: Pam Johnson
  67-69: Eileen Mueller Neill
  70-71: © Michael P. Gadomski, © Tom Myers, © Jean
    Zamenick, Photo Researchers*
  72-76: Susan Schmidt
  77-80: © Blair Seitz, Photo Researchers*; Roberta Polfus
  81: Joe McDermott
  82: Roberta Polfus
  83: © Gianni Tortoli, Science Source from Photo
    Researchers*
  84-85: Joe McDermott; © Douglas Pebbles, Index/Stock*
  86: Len Ebert
  87: Randy Chewning
  88-89: © Wesley Bocxe, Photo Researchers*; © Jordan
    Coonrad*; © Sipa Press*
  91: Lydia Halverson
  92-93: © Richard Hutchings, Photo Researchers*
  94: © Tony Rankin, The Image Bank*
  95-98: Randy Chewning
  99-102: Susan Schmidt; © Mark Boulton, Photo
    Researchers*; © Charles Mason, Black Star*;
    © Sipa Press*
  103: Len Ebert
  104-105: © Hank deLespinasse, The Image Bank*
  106-107: Pam Johnson
  108-109: Roberta Polfus
  110: Len Ebert
  111: NASA*

112-115: Michele Noiset; NASA*
117-121: Gwen Connelly
  122: Eileen Mueller Neill
  123: Maurice Snook*
  125: Roberta Polfus
  126: © Hal Stuber, Hansen Planetarium*
  127: Len Ebert
128-129: Eileen Mueller Neill
  131: NASA*
132-133: © T. A. Wiewandt, DRK Photo*
134-135: Eileen Mueller Neill
136-137: © Henry Lansford, Science Source from Photo
    Researchers*; © Tom Bean, DRK Photo*; Dick
    Canby, DRK Photo*
  138: Gwen Connelly
139-141: Randy Chewning
  142: © Stephen J. Krasemann, DRK Photo*
143-144: Randy Chewning
  145: Len Ebert
  146: © T. A. Wiewandt, DRK Photo*
147-149: Eileen Mueller Neill
151-157: Yoshi Miyake
  158: Eileen Mueller Neill
  160: NASA*
  161: Lydia Halverson
  162: © Wayne Eastep, The Stock Market*
  165: Ken Hawkins, Sygma*
166-167: Len Ebert; NASA*
  168: © C. Fuelner, The Image Bank*
  169: Len Ebert
  170: Lydia Halverson
  171: D. Cavagnaro, DRK Photo*
172-173: © Index/Stock*
174-175: Randy Chewning
  177: Yoshi Miyake; University of Chicago*
  179: University of Chicago*
  180: Len Ebert
  181: Gwen Connelly
182-183: Yoshi Miyake
184-185: Susan Schmidt
  187: © Gay Bumgarner, Index/Stock*
  188: © James Church, Index/Stock*
  189: Len Ebert
190-193: Samantha Smith
194-197: Anita Nelson
199-200: Lydia Halverson
  203: © Soames Summerhays, Photo Researchers*;
    Susan Schmidt
  204: Susan Schmidt
  205: © Jeff Foott, Tom Stack & Associates*
  206: © Doug Perrine, DRK Photo*
  207: Susan Schmidt
208-209: © H. Reinhard, OKAPIA from Photo Researchers*
210-213: Eileen Mueller Neill
  214: Len Ebert
  215: Eileen Mueller Neill
216-219: Carol Lerner
220-221: Susan Schmidt
  222: Shel Silverstein, from *A Light in the Attic*
223-224: Robert Alley
  225: © Frank J. Miller, Photo Researchers*
226-229: Joan Holub; Don & Pat Valenti, Tom Stack &
    Associates*
  230: Len Ebert
231-232: Robert Alley
  233: © John Bova, Photo Researchers*
235-240: Paige Billin-Frye
  242: © Lawrence Migdale*; © C. C. Lockwood, DRK
    Photo*
  243: NASA*; Camerique from H. Armstrong Roberts*
  244: © Derek Trask, Index/Stock*; H. Thonig,
    H. Armstrong Roberts*

Index

This index is an alphabetical list of the important topics covered in this book. It will help you find information given in both words *and* pictures. To help you understand what an entry means, there is sometimes a helping word in parentheses. For example, *booms* (oil spill). If there is information in both words and pictures, you will see the words *with pictures* after the page number. If there is *only* a picture, you will see just the word *picture* after the page number.